D1253957

INDEX

5 A very British roadster
13 The ancestor
21 Design
51 Technical description
65 Driving impressions

Publisher:
Bruno Alfieri
Editors:
Ippolito Alfieri, Alessandra Finzi
Photos:
Gabriela Noris
Graphic design:
Isabella Gianazza
Production:
Massimo Fabbri, Attilio Chiozza
Translation:
Jane Glover

ISBN 88-85880-61-4   CL 41-0249-5

La Collection®
© 1992 by Automobilia Srl
Società per la Storia e l'Immagine dell'Automobile
I-20125 Milano, via Ponte Seveso 25
All rights are reserved for all countries

PRINTED AND BOUND IN ITALY
by Grafiche Francesco Ghezzi, Milano.

AUTOMOBILIA

Bruno Alfieri

LOTUS
ELAN

A VERY BRITISH ROADSTER

The open car really flowered immediately after the war. It grafted itself on to the sudden evolution of form, a phenomenon which, being itself the product of an autonomous design culture possessed of entropy – although enlivened by the exploits of brilliant constructors and coachbuilders (Bugatti, Gangloff, Lancia, Ferdinand Porsche) – picked up the new techniques, new visual modes and innovatory culture prompted by the immense progress in aeronautics and the parallel world of rationalist forms. The Auto Union Grand Prix cars, the Cisitalia, designed under the bombs in Turin, were, there is no doubt, forerunners, but the determining factors were the recovery of the economy and of morale after World War II.

The new curved, enveloping forms, which tended towards faired-in wheels, running boards and protrusions in general, were an immediate hit with drivers. But at least four schools of car design could be identified: German, French, Italian and British.

Behind the evolution of the car in Germany, during the war, was *professor* Ferdinand Porsche. His was a global approach, working with mechanicals and bodywork together, seeing them as a unit. In a certain sense Porsche was the coachbuilders' worst enemy, and in fact no-one, not even Pinin Farina or Touring, has ever managed to "clothe" a Volkswagen or a Porsche. So much so, that when he was asked to make a suggestion on the Beetle's evolution, Pinin could only reply: "It's perfect. I suggest that they widen the rear windscreen a little". However, the brilliant *professor* Porsche was perhaps too much of an engineer, and not enough a man of visual culture. The 1954 Porsche Speedster, or the Porsche 356 Cabrio, suffer from the effects of a essential design philosophy, totally bare of any superstructure, almost barren. After Porsche, all German roadsters, including the Mercedes, had their starting points in the rather monastic severity of the Porschian forms – slightly

The Lotus Elan is the first completely new model from the prestigious British marque since 1975. It had its launch at the 1989 Motor Show in London and went on sale in February 1990.

toned down and only recently clearly denied, by the italian Bruno Sacco Head of Mercedes-Benz Styling Division.

The French roadsters have always been a compromise between miserly austerity and *joie de vivre*, between economising on materials and accessories and a certain type of *art déco* excesses. The Chapron convertible, for instance, on the Citroën DS floor-pan, an echo of Coco Chanel, or some Peugeot convertibles too, if you prefer.

The Italian roadsters (or spiders, as they call them) have always been the most tormented by the desire for harmony and smooth forms, with an un-

Forty years earlier, at the Motor Show in London, the Jaguar XK 120 made its first public appearance: the forerunner of every British roadster.

6

stoppable tendency towards the dictates (true or false) of aerodynamics. The Touring Alfa Romeo Disco Volante (1953) for instance, or the Pinin Farina 1955 Giulietta Spider, or the Ferrari 275/330 GTS by the same firm. From the Olivetti Lexicon by Marcello Nizzoli (1948) to the architecture of Ignazio Gardella or Gio Ponti, Italian

designers have always been capable of looking around them (the Baptistry at Parma in Nizzoli's case, definitely; the villas of Palladio or Michelozzo for Gardella; Mediterranean architecture for Ponti) and of giving a sense of continuity to their work.

Pre-war British roadsters were cars for

Triumph, a historic British marque, showed this 20TS prototype at the 1959 Motor Show. From it came the TR2 and successive evolutions, up to the final one, the TR7.

riding the wind on mechanicals and coachwork cobbled together, with a few notable exceptions. One was the Bentley 4 1/2-litre with compressor (1930), which also reveals clear symptoms of research. After the war, even although she was one of the big three victors, Britain endured austerity economic policies which hit the car industry hard, to the extent that stylistic evolution was less rapid than in the losing countries (Italy and West Germany). The desire for rebirth, for a dynamic life to be lived in the open air, to travel, came up against a series of outmoded products. Even halfway through the 1950s the British were driving 1930s-style roadsters, like the MG TD or TF, the Jaguar SS, the Triumph TR1 and 2. This led to the impression that the British automotive ideal was only conjugated with styling elements from the past, albeit a glorious one.

The truth of the matter was different. When exports – in practice only to the USA – began to grow healthy, money became available for new projects. All of a sudden, those roadsters were born whose lines, although extravagant, were yet stylistically appreciable, in some cases brilliant, like the Jaguar XK 120 and 150, the MGA, the Triumph TR3 and 4, the Sunbeam Alpine, the AC Cobra, the Lotus Super Seven, the Daimler SP 250, the Austin-Healey 3000 Mk III, the Morgan Plus 4 and the Frazer-Nash.

Two main characteristics stand out in all these roadsters: the extreme freedom of the designer's pen as it draws the lines: curved, straight, horizontal, vertical or oblique; and the ingenuity of certain ideas, even with regard to details. The British designers did not let problems of "family look" worry them when they were dealing with an open tourer: all they did was stick the right kind of grille on, sometimes totally different from the saloon version. The bodywork had to be always light and Spartan, but not without a touch of distinction, with well-designed seats.

As far as details were concerned, it often seemed that certain functions, such as mechanisms for opening doors, bonnet, petrol cap and glove compartment, were left to other designers, or even to chance. The MGA doors had no handles. They could be opened by slipping a hand into the map pocket inside the door and pulling a rubber-coated wire. As there were no windows, it was an easy operation. But things changed when side flaps in perspex and rainproof fabric, with a sliding window, were added, especially when the perspex used to stick in the rain. The horn button was sited in the middle of the dashboard. The only map-light was low down in front of the passenger's seat (always supposing that there was a passenger).

But the spontaneity and irrationality of the details were the most snobbishly British aspect of their cars. I do not know, and never shall, whether their success in America was due to their snob appeal or to the quantity of models on offer and the fact of being Anglo-Saxon cousins. Apart from the Jaguars, XK 120, 150 and finally

the E-Type, which the Americans genuinely liked, I have my doubts regarding their appreciation of British manias. So much so, that Nash called for Pinin Farina, to have him build the stupendous Nash-Healey, and the little Porsches went down very well in California, in Florida and on the East Coast.

The Lotus Seven was the roadster which more than any other embodied the British conception of this kind of car: small, uncomfortable and noisy, but marvellous fun. In 1973 Colin Chapman sold all rights in the car to Caterham Cars, where the car is still being produced.

If the Jaguar E-Type (1961) was the last great invention of the Roadster golden age, this Lotus Elan seems to be a return, as glorious as it is unexpected, of the ideology of the car/gadget – irrational but up-to-date, incongruous in certain details but powerful and efficient – but able, too, to take you five hundred miles in another direction, quickly, with no problems.

In the following pages we shall see why the Lotus Elan can be defined as a very British roadster.

The AC Cobra has taken its rightful place amongst the authentic automotive legends. Body and chassis were built by the British AC Cars Ltd. using Ford mechanicals. The whole thing was put together by the peerless master Carroll Shelby.

The Morgan is confirmation of the eternal success which the "classic" British roadster still enjoys today. The Plus 8 is produced on Rover mechanicals, but the body reproduces the historic British styling.

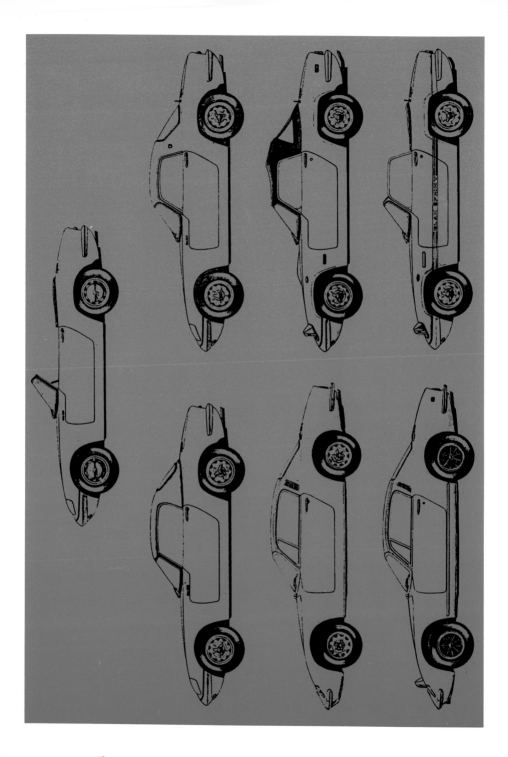

THE ANCESTOR

The Lotus Elan, launched in public at the London Motorfair in October 1989, is the first really new Lotus since the Esprit coupé designed by Giugiaro, still in production in its new versions. And it is also the first Lotus to have front-wheel drive, but it is not the first to have a plastic body: this was the little Elite coupé, in 1957, powered by the 1.2-litre Coventry Climax engine. This car, in its turn, can be considered the founding member of a family of rounded, aerodynamic shapes – helped, there is no doubt, by the material-moulding techniques – which was to be the prelude to the real ancestor of today's Elan: the 1962 Lotus Elan. Designed by Chapman, several aspects of the first Elan were revolutionary. It had a central backbone chassis in folded steel on to which the mechanicals and suspensions were mounted and, last of all, a good-looking fiberglass body. It had pop-up headlights. The engine, and this is another recurring element in the two Elans, was a 4-cylinder with two over-head camshafts: at the time it was a Ford 1498 cc, which, with a Lotus cylinder head and a compression ratio of 9.5:1, had an output of 100 HP and pushed the car up to the respectable speed of over 180 kph. Then piston displacement increased to 1600 cc.

The 1962 Elan was very successful: powerful, economical, reliable, around 15,000 were built in the different versions until 1974, enough to ensure a prolonged period of prosperity for Chapman and his business.

The top-end version was the +2, a long wheelbase coupé, which stopped production in 1973. Chapman planned it to attract a slightly older and less sporty clientele, but a richer one. It was a very elegant coupé, also clad in fibreglass, with two comfortable seats instead of almost scratch ones, although it did have a curious fault, which leads us once more to a typically British kind of design ingenuity. The cabin was not adequately ventilated and this, added to the engine's inadequ-

Versions of the Elan first series. From top to bottom, left to right: Elan 1962-1964, Elan S2 1964-1966, Elan S3 1965-1968, Elan +2 1967-1969, Elan S4 1968-1973, Elan +2S 1968-1973, Elan Sprint 1971-1973.
A total of 15,000 cars were built.

ate heat insulation, raised the temperature to unbearable levels, even in the winter. The Lotus-tuned Ford engine was delightful, roadholding was good and the brakes were excellent. Colin Chapman's monogram adorned the steering wheel.

Given the changed design conditions and with the technological development which has taken place since the Elan's time, allowing results and performance figures which were unthinkable in the old days, it is still interesting to see that the new Elan's starting point in no way differs from that of its 1962 ancestor: it is still a small, compact, open 2-seater, with a GRP body and an innovative structure, with an "external" engine of about the same size. There are two big differences though: the engine has a 4-valve-per-cylinder head and a sophisticated IHI compressor with electronic multipoint fuel injection, and it is now a front-wheel drive, in obeisance to current trands which favour simplicity of construction and ease of vehicle control.

The unusual freshness of form in the body design also indicates the new Elan's clear derivation from the 1962 model. Both Elans can be defined as precursors of a simple, quite bold design, in the modern taste. Here too it is easy to identify the "Britishness" of the design and all its details. It is a British roadster, but in the Lotus tradition: powerful and fast.

The Hethel plant where 3 models are currently in production: the Elan, the Esprit and the Excel. Lotus has been part of General Motors since 1986.

The Ellie was launched at the London Motor Show in October 1957. It was powered by a 4-cylinder 1.2-litre engine with an output of no less than 72 H.P. About 1000 were produced over the period May 1958 to March 1964.

The Elan 1st series with hard top. Initially the engine was a 4-cylinder 1.5-litre Coventry Climax, but in 1963 displacement was increased definitively to 1.6 litres.

The Elan S130 evolution of the Elan +2 was the top of the range version, both in performance and spec. Output was around 130 HP, with a top speed of over 200 kph.

The Elan Sprint was the most sporty version, powered by the same engine as the S130. Almost 1000 were built.

The Elan Sprint was also available as a soft-top, further emphasising its compact, soft lines.

The project's history

The father of the new Elan is really Michael J. Kimberley, who joined Lotus in 1969 from Jaguar, where he had been in charge of the XJ13 project, the famous rear-engined racing car which never raced. Mike Kimberley was promoted to technical director in April 1974, thanks to his proven dynamism, and the good results of his work on the little mid-engined Lotus Europa project. He is currently non-executive group chairman.

Together with Colin Spooner, Kimberley managed to convince Chapman in 1981 that Lotus ought to go back to its roots and once more build a small, innovative, 2-seater, open sports car, to replace the glorious Elan, of which roadster-version production had ended in 1973 (two years later the +2 rolled off the assembly line).

Although Colin Chapman was aiming at the more ambitious project of a 4-door saloon, he agreed as long as a component supply contract was signed with one of the big manufacturers.

After a long research by Kimberley and Spooner, it transpired that Toyota was the only car manufacturer at the time with a range of medium-sized, multivalve, dohc, advanced technology engines. Toyota was very enthusiastic about the project and in a short time the two companies achieved a degree of collaboration which was satisfactory to Kimberley and Spooner. Together they produced a new project, known as M90, which took on the concrete form of a front-engined, rear-drive, sports car with 16-valver 1600 cc and 2000 cc engines and two overhead camshafts.

Following Chapman's death at the end of 1982, and the sudden financial difficulties which ensued, the project was suspended. It was only taken up again in November 1983, when construction of a running prototype started, to end in March of the following year.

Two years after the completion of the original project, they found themselves

Two different philosophies flow together in the Elan II series: tradition and innovation. It is a typically British roadster, with very sophisticated, avantgarde mechanicals. It was the first front-wheel drive Lotus.
Above, the traditional badge with Anthony Colin Bruce Chapman's initials.

success at the London Motorfair in October 1984.

Before giving the go-ahead to the X100 project, the technical decision was made to build the new Elan with front-wheel drive. This was in line with market trends, and since Lotus had done considerable development work on the drivability and manageability of front-wheel drive cars for other constructors, it was logical that the project of the little Lotus would benefit from the degree of technology attained, setting new standards worldwide.

It was January 1985, and by the end of the summer of the same year the three-door and convertible versions had been designed and approved. The styling and development phases were next, but in February 1986 General Motors acquired control of Lotus following negotiations conducted by Alan Curtis, the new chairman of Group Lotus.

Planning requirements and circumstances had changed once again and the X100 project was re-examined by the board of Lotus. Although the car was a good project, Kimberley abandoned it in March 1986. Creating an outstanding sports car for the 1990s required a clean start.

Eight months later, in November 1986, a presentation was made to the board of a model, without an engine, and approved. In February 1987 a ten-year agreement

faced with a change in market demand which necessitated a new body style for the M90. In the meantime, David Wickens had become majority shareholder at Lotus and it was decided that the X100 – the new car's codename – would have the same bodywork lines as the "Etna" project which had been shown to great

Three-quarter front views of the Lotus Elan. The lines of the frontal are soft and free from any sharp edges. The self-colour bumper wraps the car right up to the wheelarches, protecting it from small knocks.

The lights clusters are retractable. Each element has two lamps, one beam and one dipped.
The retractable headlamps can also be operated manually in the event of a fault.
The rearview mirrors (opposite page) are electrically adjusted and self-defrosting.

ish Design Council.

With two thirds of production destined for export we see the Elan as being a flagship worldwide for Lotus technology.

Although the story of the history of the Elan project was long and went through difficult times, including the death in 1982 of Colin Chapman, the Lotus team's tenacity successfully created the "real heir" to the best-loved Lotus of all time. It is as the Lotus Press Office says, "You have never driven a car like the new Lotus Elan because there has never been a car like it".

The bodywork

The Lotus Elan is a car with the spirit of a gadget, which strikes the eye because of its imaginative and unconventional bodywork, but which, as we shall see further on, conceals highly respectable technical contents which make it a powerful, fast, safe vehicle. It is a strict two-seater, but provides ample space for driver and passenger. The layout of the mechanicals – front transverse engine and front-wheel drive – made it possible to design a very compact car, 3.803 m long and 1.734 m wide (without mirrors). It is 1.23 m high with the hood up, and weighs 1020 kg (Turbo SE) and 997 kg (SE). The Cd is 0.34 with the hood up or 0.38 down. The sensation of enormous compactness is accentuated by the tail,

was signed with Isuzu, the Japanese manufacturer, to supply a new high-powered engine, still in the design phase, and the car's launch-date was fixed for within the end of 1989.

Following its first year on the UK market, the Lotus Elan won the prestigious Design Award presented by the Brit-

Three-quarter rear views of the Elan. The horizontal light clusters are rather conventional looking. The numberplate has a plastic protection strip.

From this angle the original sloping cut of the tail stands out. The small spoiler is one of the most successful bits of the Elan. The bumper is heavier, more pronounced, than the front one.

The steeply raked windscreen, the smooth body panels, the negative-lift frontal, all conspire to give the car a good Cd (0.38 with the roof down, 0.34 closed). The handles (opposite page) are hidden in a small aperture flush to the door rabbet.

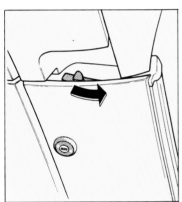

Frontal views of the Elan with lamps open and closed. Vents draw air to the inter-cooler, radiator, air-conditioner and front brakes.

which descends brusquely, but in a curved line, towards the ground.

The frontal reveals a family relationship with the Lotus Esprit – although the taut Italianised lines of the latter are counterbalanced by the softer, fuller, ones of the Elan. The flanks are smooth, but here too, the Elan looks more rounded. The winds-creen inclines steeply back from the curved frame at the bottom, which is set well forward. This provides more cabin space but penalises forward visibility if you do not want to place the seat nearer to the steering wheel. This is made worse by the position of the sunshades which are mounted too far inside the windscreen frame, and are so large, that when folded up they intrude into the field of vision. If they are not taken off, like in the old roadsters, they need moving higher up, to reduce the overhanging surface area: it is quite an easy modification. The outer rear-view mirrors are pretty, so are the wheel rims whose swollen crown is well-matched to the form's overall curvy compactness.

The inside of the Elan, with its vivacious fabric or leather trim, is very pleasing to look at and, I would add, enjoyable. Everything has a look of modern design about it, but one does breathes a residue, at least, of British style, and welcome it is, too. From the seats to the instruments, from the steering wheel to the facia, from the gear-lever to the glove compartment, the roadster brilliantly conserves the warmth which was typical of the inside of an MGA or the Triumph TRs or the Austin-Healey Hundred. There is a slim vein of humour, or complicity with the driver, if you prefer, which is a good way away from the Beethovian functionalism

of the Mercedes or the Audis, or from the "beauty for beauty's sake" of the Italians or from the "enjoy yourself, because what I'm giving you is the best going" of the Japanese, Mazda Miata included. For those who want the details, what follows is a detailed analysis of the cabin.

A well-stocked dash in front of the dr-iver provides good visibility of on-board instrumentation; secondary controls are easy to find. There is a cubby in front of the passenger, and an object tray in the central console, along with the electric controls for the windows and the outside rear-view mirrors, and there are elasti-cated map pockets too, if required. The instrument panel has analog dials with anti-glare glass and red numbers and ne-edles on a black background; a speedo calibrated to 260 kph, a tacho to 8000 rpm and fuel, water temperature, voltmeter and oil pressure gauges, are all standard. In the turbo models the analog clock has been replaced by the air feed pressure gauge and a digital clock.

There are eleven indicator/warning lights along the bottom edge of the instru-ment panel which are invisible until they light up. There are two courtesy lights un-der the inside rear-view mirror, with in-dependent switches and a delayed ac-tion device, operated by the door.

We come now to the hood, an essential part of every roadster. The controls for both opening/closing the hood panel and the petrol cap cover are centrally located inside, for increased security and the boot can only be opened with the key. The manually-operated, fabric-lined hood folds away into a bay behind the seats, with a lid flush to the body panels. When the hood is raised it fastens onto the wind-

Rear shots of the Elan. The luggage compartment is small, as is often the case in this kind of car.

screen easily, with two hooks.

To complete this analysis of the Lotus Elan's bodywork, it is important to underline the advanced construction methods used for the body panels themselves, and their paint job. The roadster's "skin" is produced by a process of vacuum-assisted resin injection (VARI), which involves using a greater number of separate panels.

Lotus Engineering came up with a new patented process of "fibre molds", to produce pre-formed fibreglass reinforcement which is placed directly inside the VARI moulds during pressing.

At the same time as this work was going on, different adhesives were evaluated, including the epoxy resins and rigid acrylic urethanes which were being used in the car industry at the time. The results showed that modular elastomeric polyurethane was the ideal adhesive.

At the beginning of the 1980s Lotus developed the VARI process, using resins which remained stable during polymerisation, to ensure dimensional stability and the absence of surface warping. Although the stable resins had been available since 1970, they required a molding temperature of 150°C, which was not compatible with the VARI process.

Research, therefore, was directed towards a stable resin which could be molded at a more acceptable temperature of 55°C. Lotus looked at a material produced by Ashland Chemicals of Columbus, Ohio, which met their requirements and this led to the development of a new production process for the Elan.

A further improvement came from the

The hood is very small and discreet and does not "contaminate" the Elan's soft, dynamic lines.

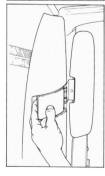

An illustration of the hood operating procedure: after releasing the two hooks at the top of the windscreen (above) the hood is lifted and folded into the bay, opened by a handle set in the right door-pillar (below).

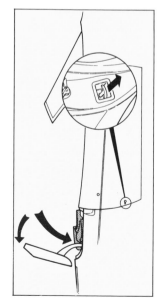

The Elan Turbo SE cockpit. Very functional with extremely legible, well-sited instrumentation and indicators. Two people, even slightly over average size, can be seated in comfort. But that is all.
Right, the instrument panel with red figures on black dials.

nickel-plated shell production molds, which not only increase the life of the equipment itself, but provide a high-quality finishing for the body panels, reducing pre-painting preparation to a minimum. There is effectively no shrinkage during the polymerisation process, ensuring optimal dimensional control.

In addition it was possible, using fibreglass reinforcing, to design panels with relatively sharp corners.

All the outer body panels have a nominal thickness of 2 mm, as their function is purely aesthetical, not load bearing, but there are some exceptions. The apron, bulkheads, bumper armatures and the inner door-panels have been designed thicker to improve structural quality.

All Elans have RRIM bumpers front and back, similar to the ones on current Esprit models. The car has an energy-absorbing front bumper in accordance with US federal law.

The shape of the outer door panels prevents the usage of normal hinges, and a unique design has been used, allowing the doors to rotate in an arc outside the front A panel, instead of inside it. On the extremity of the door locks is a specially-designed, conical, automatic safety device, which means that in the event of a side impact the lower door member intrudes towards the lock and from here towards the main car structure.

Close-up of the secondary indicators on the dash and central air vents.

Below, on the left, the wheel, with the historic Lotus badge. On the right, the cubby on the passenger side.

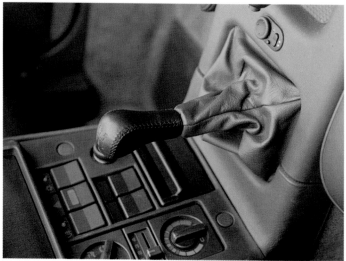

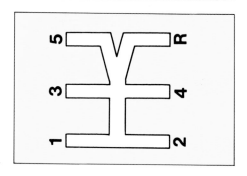

Cabin details. From the left: gear lever, central console with handbrake and electric window controls, the belt take-up and the map pocket on the door.

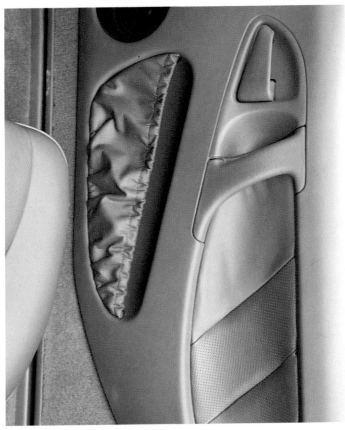

The dashboard on a right-hand drive Elan is slightly different from the left-hand version. (See p. 48-49).

Several different trims are available for the Elan, in fabric and hide. This is a right-hand drive with twin-tone leather trim, in characteristic British taste.

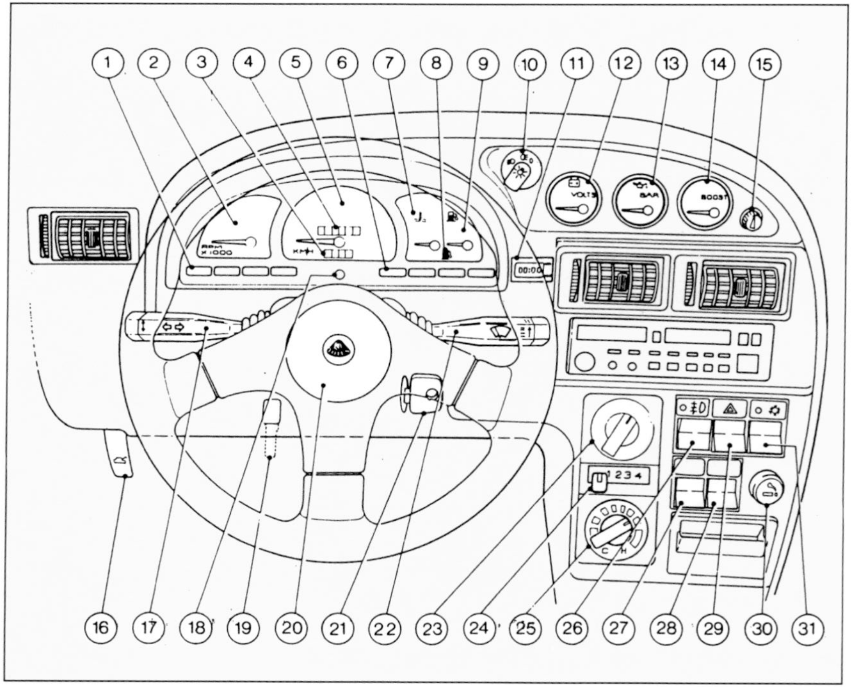

INSTRUMENTS AND CONTROLS
Left-hand drive

1 - Left hand tell tale bank
2 - Tachometer
3 - Trip distance recorder
4 - Total distance recorder
5 - Speedometer
6 - Right hand tell tale bank
7 - Water temperature gauge
8 - Low fuel tell tale
9 - Fuel gauge
10 - Main lighting switch
11 - Digital clock (Turbo)
12 - Voltmeter
13 - Oil pressure gauge
14 - Boost gauge (Turbo) or analogue clock (N.A.)
15 - Panel illumination rheostat
16 - Bonnet release lever
17 - Beam/dip & turn indicators
18 - Trip reset knob
19 - Column height clamp lever
20 - Horn button
21 - Ignition/starter/steering lock
22 - Windscreen wash/wipe control
23 - Airflow distribution control
24 - Fan speed switch
25 - Heater temperature control
26 - Rear fog lamps switch
27 - Switch blank
28 - Switch blank
29 - Hazard warning lights switch
30 - Cigar lighter
31 - Air conditioning switch

48

INSTRUMENTS AND CONTROLS
Right-hand drive

1 - Boost gauge (Turbo) or analogue clock (N.A.)
2 - Oil pressure gauge
3 - Panel illumination rheostat
4 - Voltmeter
5 - Left hand tell tale bank
6 - Tachometer
7 - Trip reset knob
8 - Trip distance recorder
9 - Total distance recorder
10 - Speedometer
11 - Right hand tell tale bank
12 - Water temperature gauge
13 - Low fuel tell tale
14 - Fuel gauge
15 - Windscreen wash/wipe control
16 - Air conditioning switch
17 - Cigar lighter
18 - Hazard warning lights switch
19 - Rear fog lamps switch
20 - Heater temperature control
21 - Fan speed switch
22 - Airflow distribution control
23 - Switch blank
24 - Switch blank
25 - Digital clock (Turbo)
26 - Beam/dip & turn indicators
27 - Column height clamp lever
28 - Horn button
29 - Ignition/starter/steering lock
30 - Main lighting switch
31 - Bonnet release lever

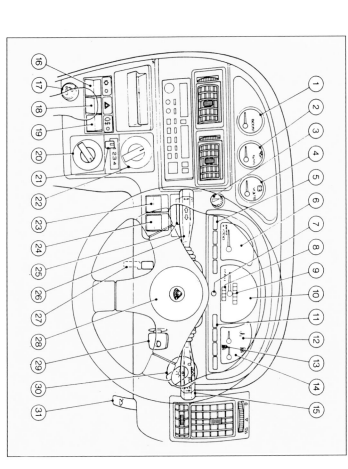

Engines

The Elan's engine, which has "Isuzu-Lotus" stamped on its cam-boxes, was developed, as this wording suggests, by the two companies and is built by Isuzu at their factory in Hokkaido, Japan. It should not be forgotten that Isuzu is one of the car-makers of which General Motors is a majority shareholder. It is a 1588 cc 16-valve 4 in-line, with an output of 132 HP at 7200 rpm in the unblown version, and 167 HP at 6600 rpm in the SE version with turbo and intercooler. The torque figures for both engines are 142 Nm and 200 Nm at 4200 rpm respectively. Top engine speed is 7600 rpm in the normally aspirated version and 7000 rpm in the turbo.

The engine is an iron block/aluminium head unit with 4 valves per cylinder. Two overhead camshafts driven by toothed-belt operate the valves by self-regulating hydraulic gear. Bore and stroke are 80 mm and 79 mm.

Compression ratios are 10.0:1 in the un-blown engine and 8.2:1 in the turbo model. The latter has an IHI turbo with 0.65 supercharging. Both engines have DELCO electronic management systems, designed to Lotus specifications and Rochester fuel injection. The turbo engine also has a DELCO electronic ignition system with no distributor.

In accordance with British law, both engines will run on unleaded and ordinary fuel with respective octane ratings of 95 and 97, without any need to adjust or recalibrate engine electronics. For the US and European markets which require a catalyst, the engines are calibrated to use unleaded fuel with an octane rating of 97.

Transmission

Both models have a transaxle 5-gear mechanical gearbox with normal ratios. However, the turbo version has a higher final drive ratio of 3.833:1 against the 4.117:1 of the normal version, which produces a top speed of 220 kph in the former and 196 kph in the latter version.

The Elan has two 1.6-litre Isuzu power-plants. The normally aspirated version has an output of 137 HP at 7200 rpm, the turbocharged version (photographed here) has an output of 167 HP at 6600 rpm.

In order to compensate the turbo engine's greater power and torque, there is a 225 mm clutch, compared to a 215 mm one on the lower-powered model.

Chassis

Lotus took the decision not to give the Elan a simple chassis, opting instead for a unitary composite construction of floorpan and backbone chassis.

The determining factor in this decision was the technical requirements involved in building a very stiff convertible. The Elan's floorpan consists of a single vacuum resin injection with a nominal thickness of 3 mm. This mold is then riveted and joined to the reinforced steel cradle which includes: inner door sills, front and rear members and front and central pillars. When fixed to the back-bone chassis, torsional stiffness of 8950 Nm is achieved, an extraordinarily high value for a convertible, and it is this which determines the car's exceptional handling characteristics.

The floorpan is made from continuous filament fibreglass based on isophthalic polyester resin, reinforced in certain areas subjected to heavy loads, such as joins between the monocoque and the chassis and the area which bears the fuel tank. The brake and pedal mounting points are built using the same technique.

The cradle and front and central posts

Both engines have double overhead camshafts and four valves per cylinder.

are in 18 mm steel, painted and waxed before assembly to maximise protection from corrosion. Elastomeric polyurethane–based adhesives are used in production. These steel components do not only contribute to the car's flexibility and torsional stiffness, but provide stiffened mounting points for the seat runners, for the lower belt-anchorage points and the door hinges.

Additional structural stiffening and protection from side impacts is supplied by transverse steel supports located between the front and rear pillars.

The backbone chassis extends rearwards from the front bulkhead, and includes the rear suspension mounting points, with the side member/subframe group – with pick-up points for the front suspension, engine bearings and front-impact absorbing structure – in front. The whole subframe, including the power-train, is detachable, to ease construction and maintenance.

High-resistance cast aluminium is used for the windscreen pillars which are mounted directly above the front pillar, joined by an extruded aluminium bar.

Suspensions

When it was decided to make the new Elan the first front-wheel drive Lotus, an intense research programme was started to make sure that the car kept up Lotus old tradition, by attaining new world

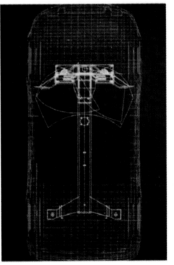

Two CAD/CAM studies for the Elan chassis.

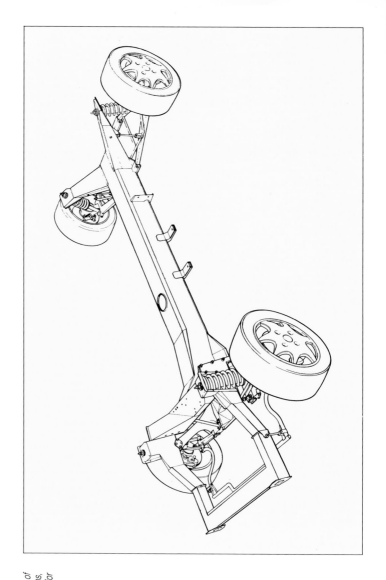

The Elan's steel backbone chassis. One of Colin Chapman's many genial inventions, it has been a feature of Lotus cars for many years.

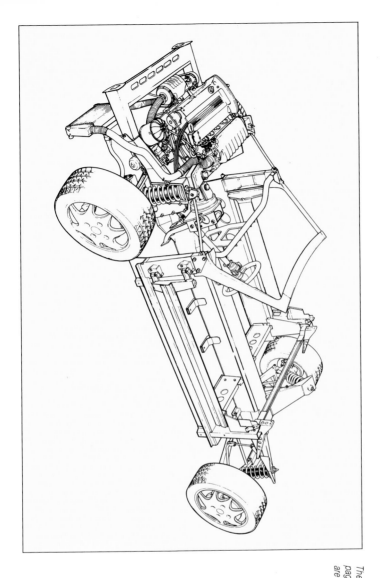

The backbone chassis (see opposite page) is fixed to the floorpan. The A-pillars are in steel.

55

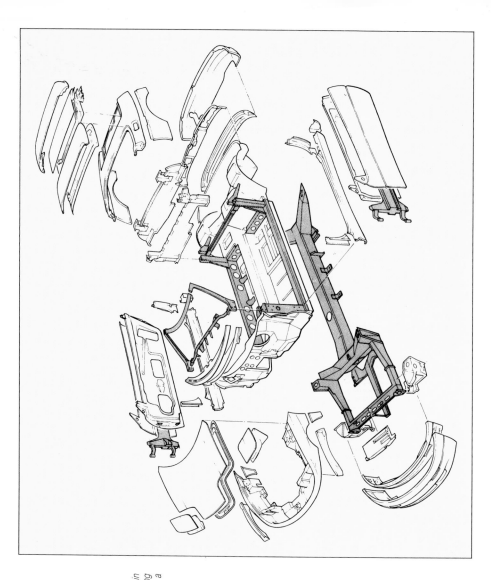

The outer body panels. More than fifty in number, they are only 2 mm thick, having a purely aesthetic function rather than a load-bearing one.

standards in handling, roadholding and stability in this class of sports cars too.

The need for longitudinal suppleness without sacrificing steering precision, handling and traction, impossible with normal types of suspension, was obvious right from the first X100 prototypes.

So a completely new system of interactive wishbone suspensions were designed by Roger Becker, John Miles and Jerry Booen. Each front-wheel group is attached to a separate structure in heat-treated aluminium.

This structure has five main advantages:
1. It permits the use of very stiff bushes on the wishbones for accurate wheel control, without the consequent problem of excessive road noise being transmitted into the car body.
2. It permits a very low caster angle, which not only reduces steering effort at any speed, but also minimises changes in steering effort at maximum steering angle.
3. It exerts accurate control over suspension geometry in all conditions.
4. It helps reduce the effects of imprecise steering.
5. It maintains longitudinal adherence without affecting handling.

It is worth remembering that with traditional wishbones, the the bending of the bushes during braking changes the caster angle with relation to the chassis.

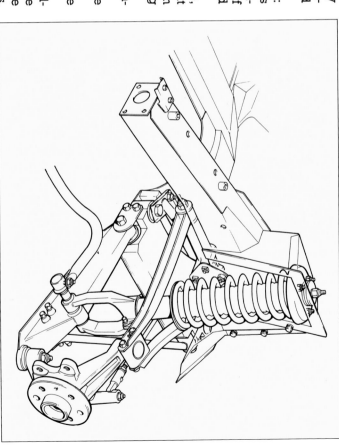

Front suspension with Lotus's new interactive double wishbones.

57

The balls joints on the upper and lower connecting rods move in opposite directions – the upper conrod moving forward and the lower one backward.

Stability while braking is improved by moving the wheel hub backwards from the steering axis.

For better running stability, camber variation is carefully constructed along the suspension's vertical movement. The same values of camber variation are applied to both front and rear suspensions, to obtain the same characteristics on bends at both ends of the vehicle and at all roll angles.

To attain progressive handling with increasing lateral acceleration, suspension geometry has been designed to provide contant chassis and trim height (30 mm in front and 60 mm in the rear) without altering the car's roll angle. Due to the Elan's short wheelbase, in relation to the height of the suspended mass's centre of gravity, a system to control dive when braking was required. So 10% of the anti-dive system was built into the front suspensions and a small part of the anti-lift system at the rear.

There are double tube shock absorbers front and rear. The Elan's double wishbone suspensions allow a less-steeply inclined stub axle, which reduces steering effort when turning.

Different Ackermann values were ex-

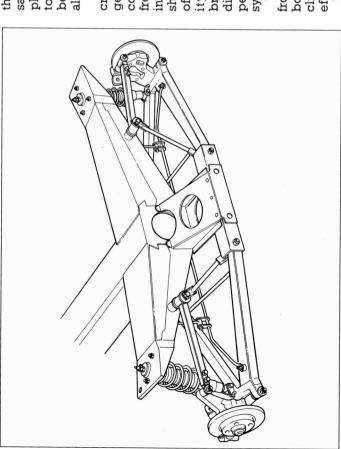

Rear suspension attached directly to the backbone chassis.

The test phase is long and laborious, as the car in question is a roadster. It was conducted for the most part on the private circuit at Millbrook.

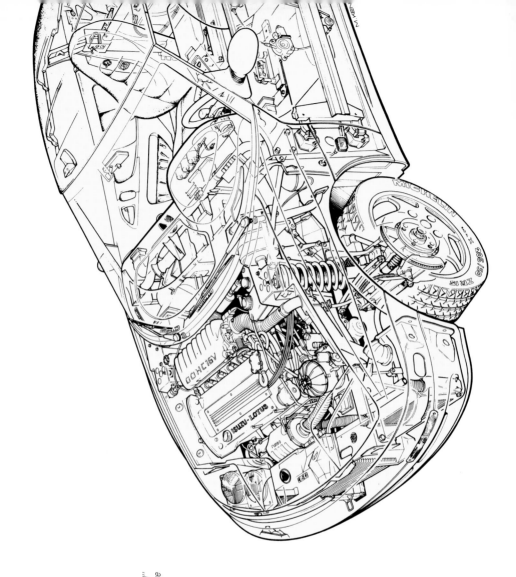

X-ray of the Elan. Note the "all-forward" architecture: typical of front-wheel drive but anomalous in this type of car.

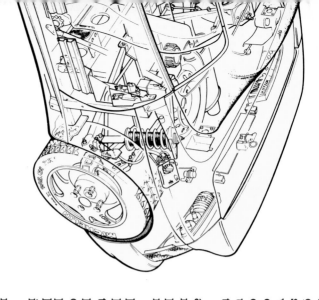

amined: high values produced excellent grip on tight bends with a slight loss of stability on fast, open bends. Lower values produced greater stability at higher speeds but, inevitably, wear and loss of grip on tight turns. It was decided to use 60% Ackermann geometry, for a better dynamic balance.

There is a 22 mm diam. tubular roll bar at the front and a solid 14 mm one at the rear. Both have ball joints to reduce the play associated with rubber bushes to the minimum.

The rear independent suspensions with links at the top and wide-based wishbones underneath are similar to those on the Excel, but have been adapted to producing 3,000 Elans and to its different design. All models have Adwest rack and pinion steering, with 3.1 turns lock to lock in manual models and 2.9 in the assisted version.

A three year unlimited mileage warranty was recently introduced, which demonstrates confidence in products and in the achievements of Lotus Cars Ltd, Lotus Engineering and Millbrook Proving Ground Ltd.

The Lotus Elan is a car in which 90 per cent of owners can enjoy 90 per cent of its performance for 90 per cent of the time: a true car of the '90's.

ELAN SE

ENGINE

Disposition: front longitudinal
Materials: cast-iron crankcase, light alloy cylinder head
Cylinders: 4 in-line
Bore and stroke: 80x79 mm (3.14x3.11 in)
Piston displacement: 1588 cc (96.9 cu in)
Compression ratio: 8.2:1
Maximum power: 123 kW (167 HP) at 6600 rpm
Maximum torque: 200 Nm (20.5 kgm) at 4200 rpm
Timing system: DOHC, 4 valves per cylinder
Fuel feed: electronic injection, IHI turbocharger with intercooler
Lubrication: forced-feed
Cooling system: cooling liquid
Emission control system: 3-way catalytic converter

DRIVELINE

Drive: front-wheel
Clutch: dry single-plate, ⌀ 225 mm
Gearbox: 5-speed + Rev mechanic
Gear ratios: 1st = 3.333, 2nd = 1.916, 3rd = 1.333, 4th = 1.027 5th = 0.829, Rev = 3.583
Final ratio: 3.833
Differential: free

CAR BODY

Type: 2-seater sports convertible
Frame: rigid steel backbone
Front suspensions: unequal length wishbones, coaxial coil springs and dampers, anti-roll bar
Rear suspensions: wide-based lower wishbone and upper link, coaxial coil springs and dampers, anti-roll bar
Steering system: rack-and-pinion, power assisted, steering ⌀ 10.6 m
Brakes: discs (front self-vented), front and rear ⌀ 256/236 mm (10/9.2 in)
Rims: 6.5J x 15, light alloy
Tyres: 205/50 ZR 15
Fuel tank: 46 lt (10.2 imp.gal.)

DIMENSIONS AND WEIGHTS:

Length: 3803 mm (149.7 in)
Width: 1734 mm (68.6 in)
Height: 1230 mm (48.4 in)
Wheelbase: 2250 mm (88.6 in)
Front and rear tracks: 1486/1486 mm (58.5/58.5 in)
Kerb weight: 1020 kg (2266 lbs)

PERFORMANCE

Top speed: 220 kph (136 mph)
Acceleration from 0 to 100 kph: 7.2 sec
400 m from standing start: 15.4 sec
Speed per 1000 rpm (5th gear): 33.6 kph
Consumption at 90/120/Urban Cycle: 6.7/8.9/10.8 lt/100 km
Specific power: 105 HP/lt (1.72 HP/cu in)
Weight to power ratio: 6.1 kg/HP (13.5 lbs/HP)

ELAN

as Elan SE, except:

ENGINE
Compression ratio: 10:1
Maximum power: 97 kW (132 HP) at 7200 rpm
Maximum torque: 142 Nm (14.5 kgm) at 4200 rpm

DRIVELINE
Clutch: dry single-plate, Ø 215 mm
Final ratio: 4.117

CAR BODY
Tyres: 205/50 VR 15

DIMENSIONS AND WEIGHTS:
Kerb weight: 997 kg (2215 lbs)

PERFORMANCE
Top speed: 196 kph (122 mph)
Acceleration from 0 to 100 kph: 8.2 sec
400 m from standing start: 16.1 sec
Speed per 1000 rpm (5th gear): 31.2 kph
Consumption at 90/120/Urban Cycle: 6.9/8.0/10.9
lt/100 km
Specific power: 83.1 HP/lt (1.36 HP/cu in)
Weight to power ratio: 7.5 kg/HP (16.7 lbs/HP)

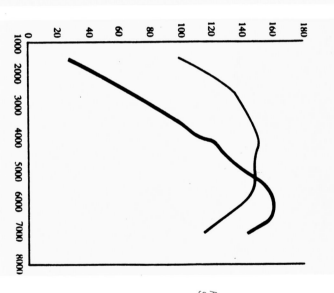

Power and torque curves of the Isuzu 1.6
SE engine.

Driving a Lotus Elan, its turbo and un-blown versions, is a unique pleasure. It is fun from the start, as soon as you get into the car and sit in the comfortable seat in front of a nicely-styled steering wheel with the Lotus badge in the middle, uncon-ventionally-designed controls (the lights, for example, are operated by a button on the dashboard), dials with red numbers and needles, and the stubby, leather-clothed gear lever.

I drove the powerful SE first, with its IHI Japanese turbo, a well-known make which equips some of the best known Italian GTs. The engine fires up straight away with a delightful, restrained, rumble. It can deliver no less than 167 HP at 6600 rpm, which is a lot for a 1588 cc four cylinder, even with 4 valves per cylinder. The comparison with the Saab 9000 turbo comes naturally. It has a not unsimilar engine, but it is a 2-litre which delivers 173 HP at top revs.

There is a surprise straight away: the engine's liveliness and drive, even at low speeds and at 1000-1500 rpm. The car, which after all weighs 1000 kg, is always docilely ready to unload its power at any engine speed, something you notice with relief and with pleasure when overtaking, even starting from low speed. Obviously, this engine is the result of punctilious, perfectionist, tuning.

The gears of the 5-speed manual 'box engage precisely and with ease. The road is devoured with that hard-to-des-cribe sensation of being immersed in the landscape, which is the fundamental fea-ture of a roadster. The engine is exube-rant, always ready to deliver more.

Steering is easy and the car is always under control. One could be induced to worry about roadholding and handling, seeing as shedding 167 HP through the front wheels alone might seem a difficult task. Instead of which, and only a very lit-tle practice is required, the Elan SE proves to be neutral, thanks also to its Michelin MXX2 205/50 ZR 15 tyres, which roll along without any noise and without

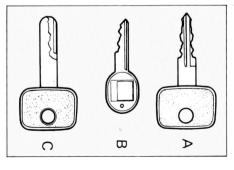

The Elan SE and the Elan have respective top speeds of 220 kph and 196 kph. Below, the three equipment keys: ignition/steering block (A), doors (B) and cubby (C).

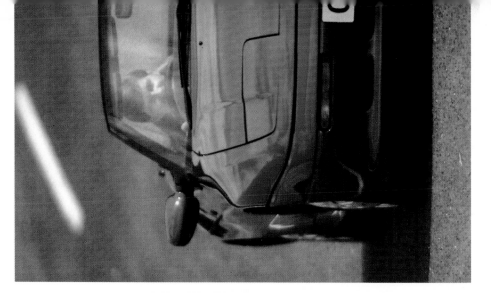

tiring the driver's arms. Nor is accelerating on bends any worry, if the road surface is decent, and I will remind you that 100 kph comes up from rest on the straight in 7.2 seconds: some feat for a 1.6-litre!

The rumble increases slightly – it is an open car – if you floor the pedal in fifth, and the speedometer needle moves resolutely towards 200. Then it has the effrontery to go on, reaching and passing 220. In front of me the motorway seems to have become narrower, and the trees shoot past at the sides, all bent.

At high speeds the situation in the cabin is as follows: with the hood up, there is a quiver which starts at about 120 kph and progressively increases. At 220 kph a roar travels through the hood. Although this can be pleasing, it prevents any conversation except by bellowing. With the top down and the side windows up, the wind causes no particular problems up to 120 kph, and continues not to, is in fact entertaining, when accelerating or overtaking at up to 150-180 kph. The hood is well made but perhaps a little on the light side, even though it has four layers of fabric, the last one waterproof. On the other hand the king of today's roadsters, the Mercedes-Benz SL, can be seen as the enjoyment of luxury and of tranquillity up to 130-150 with the hood up, 120 with it down: of course, you

One authoritative British publication maintains that the Elan, together with the Porsche 911 and the Lancia Delta Integrale, are the fastest cars from A to B-i.e. from one point to another on any kind of road. This is more than likely, especially in light of how difficult it is to use supercars like the Ferrari F40 and the Lamborghini Diablo, however fast and powerful, in normal traffic conditions.

can go up to 250, but for short distances (and it would be advisable to use the hard top on long journeys.)

Braking in both versions of the Elan is powerful and sure, even without ABS, as long as you exert a certain degree of pressure on the pedal. This is surprising when you think that the principal Lotus shareholder is GM, American right to the marrow, and the Americans like to "nail" the brakes. Fuel consumption figures are good.

One leaves the small, powerful SE, a real jewel of British design, technology and culture, with real regret.

The unblown Elan has "only" 132 HP and puts up 8.2 seconds from 0-100 kph. The engine is in fact more compressed (10:1) and is suppler than the SE's. But top speed, due amongst other things to the final drive ratio, is near 200 kph (196 to be exact) and there is still an exuberance of power, although one misses the thrust of the over boost. There is no difference in road manners.

Roadsters, even sophisticated and powerful ones like the two Elans, ought to be used for pure enjoyment and not for dreary journeys from A to B. Drive inside the landscape, enjoy the hood, accelerate and burn it up or pootle along, or make journeys to remember, like in the old days. The Lotus Elan has been designed and built for these very things. And it keeps all its promises. Happy driving!

The hard top with a heated rear windscreen, courtesy lights and Senotex trim has been available since spring 1992. But it is with the top down (below) that the Elan gives of its best.

69

The Elan colour range.

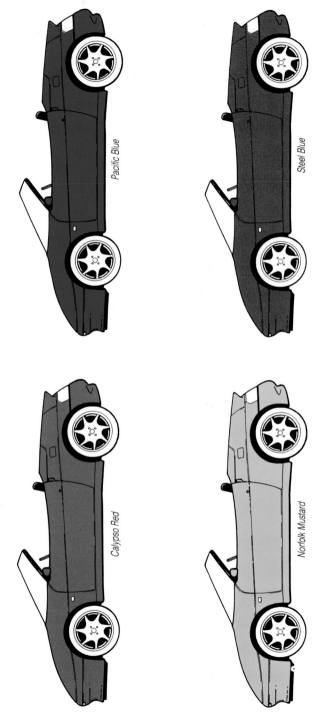

Calypso Red

Norfolk Mustard

Pacific Blue

Steel Blue

Black

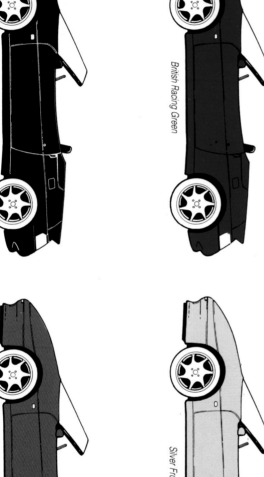

British Racing Green

Monaco White

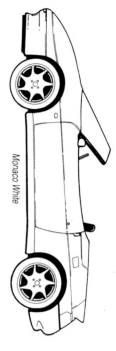

Silk Red

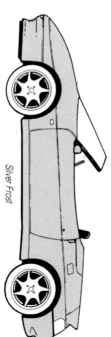

Silver Frost

Aqua Blue

Automobilia wishes to thank Lotus Cars Ltd. Hethel, Norwich, Autoexpó of Ora (Bolzano) and Motor Racing Publications of London for allowing the use of documentary material.